ESCAPE

MY JOURNEY BACK TO ME

By Doritha Skinner

Copyright 2019
Doritha Skinner

TABLE OF CONTENTS

Introduction 1

Domestic Violence 3

The Change 4

Exit Plan 36

Aftermath 40

Faith & Spirituality 45

The Now 52

Quotes – Daily Affirmations 56

Thank You 59

INTRODUCTION

As I start this journey to become someone that I have always wanted to become (ME), I am so thankful and grateful for these past few years. You see, most people have to go through something for their breakthrough. It's how you ESCAPE it that makes you complete. Going through different trials and tribulations, I began to think every human being will at least encounter something once they want to escape from. Something in your life is going to happen where you are going to feel at your all-time low. When you're going through challenges, you may not understand what you should be doing with your life. You may have an idea of how you have envisioned your future, but our Creator is the only one who knows from start to finish how our life stories will began and end.

People will remember how you take these challenges you face and turn them into the best version of yourself, how you rise and stand back up. For me personally I think about the reason why I am here on this earth. What purpose does God want me to fulfill? *And we know that in all things God works for the good of those who love him, who have been called according to his purpose.* Romans 8:28 NIV. This is a story about my journey. I didn't realize the situation I was in or how it affected me and those around me until I was deep in it. This is how I Escaped and finally discovered the real me.

I am hoping that it encourages you to ESCAPE whatever is holding you back from becoming the best version of YOU

DOMESTIC VIOLENCE

Everybody knows these words, but nobody thinks it will ever happen to them. No one thinks about the bad things – when you think love, family, your job etc. Negative thoughts are not your priority. The average person thinks "that won't happen to me," or "I'm not going to let something like that happen to me."

Unfortunately, abuse, sadness, depression, and loneliness don't have a preference. It doesn't matter what race, gender, or economic status you are. You might think your life is going well and that nothing bad will ever happen, but you still may need to ESCAPE from something.

THE CHANGE

Everyone has a story, and they're all different. For everyone, there is that one thing that makes them into the person they currently are. Unfortunately, for some of us, that thing makes us vulnerable to dangers we don't even know are out there until we're involved in them.

I never wanted to be rich or famous. All I ever wanted was to grow up to be a secretary for a big corporation, a wife and a mother. I didn't stop to think that my situation growing up might cause me problems in achieving those goals while being happy.

I grew up in a single parent home with one sibling, my twin brother. My parents divorced when my brother and I were two. All I know of what happened between my parents was what we were told. My father didn't appear in my life persistently until my twenties and then there wasn't enough time to get to know him. Cancer took him before he reached the age of 64.

The void of not having an adult man was real. My mother always said, "Pray for a good man," but she never went into detail of what to exactly ask for. When

I prayed for a good man, what specifics do I ask for? Well God is God and He knows all, so I assumed when I prayed for a good man, He would know what I meant.

At times, I still wonder if my mother's heart ever healed from her first heartbreak; my father. I stopped searching and I stopped trying to fill that void of a missing father with those unnecessary things of different substances, distractions and wanted to focus on me. I wasn't sure what that meant though. I thought that if I just stopped the things I was doing, that would be focusing on me. I was in my early twenties and had no idea who I was. I knew there was more out there for me; I just needed to find what it was.

In your twenties, I believe it is hard to find out who you are exactly, but it is a great age to start focusing on what you want in your future. Some people can figure it out right away, while others spend a lifetime trying to figure it out.

I took about a year where I was single and had time to learn about me. I was a student and a basketball manager at the local community college and another student asked if I would like to attend a birthday party in New York. I'd always dreamed of living there, and I jumped on the chance to go there and have fun.

The birthday boy was tall chocolate guy named X-Man (not his real name of course). I was taken to a place of emotions that I had not felt in a while. At first, I was too nervous to speak to him, but I knew that I couldn't be there without speaking. He had a girlfriend who certainly had his attention. I enjoyed myself and after a few beverages, I did approach him to say, "happy birthday."

A few months after that party, this same guy ended up attending the community college I was attending. I still felt those butterflies and wasn't sure completely why, but I had to ignore them because he had a girlfriend. I also wasn't sure X-Man was what I wanted. Over time, we became friends. We had the same interest in basketball and other sports, and that gave us a lot to talk about. We flirted, but nothing more. Then I noticed him acting differently with girls, and I wondered what happened to this girlfriend that he was so in love with? When I found out that they had broken up, I just continued to act the same towards him.

Does anyone in their early twenties take their lives and their actions seriously? We should, but a lot of times our actions can have us in a place where we may look back later in life and say, why did I do that?

Our college won the championship basketball game! There was a party to celebrate, and I was asked to pick X-Man up. He lived near me, but the house where he lived had no phone service. This was 2002, everybody didn't have a cell phone back then. The only way I could let him know I could take him to the party was to go over there. I was nervous. No one likes someone just showing up at their door. I went there late afternoon just to say, "Hey I can take you to the party later if you want." I was asked to come in and I didn't leave until it was time to go to the party. I did not completely let all the butterflies take over, but after talking for a few hours and noticing that we had more things in common, we ended up becoming intimate. We were inseparable from that point on.

We were college students, which meant there were no elaborate dates. I'm talking the Pizza Hut type of first date. I am a simple girl; I didn't need fancy materialistic things to turn me on. I was glad to just spend time with him.

We were young (twenty-one) and we were serious. Right?? So serious we ended up asking my mom if he could come stay with us because he wanted to finish school in Delaware and not go back to living in New York. Now, my mother is a strong Methodist woman, and my grandfather was even stricter. I thought I would just ask her, but I just knew her response would be "No!" To our complete surprise, she said "Yes." The first thought that crossed my mind was "Is this meant to be? Is this relationship really meant to be?"

I thought that if she approved, maybe this is serious. I guess his charming talk got to her too. Both of us were in college and working jobs at the same time, trying to make our futures better. Apparently, she felt that this was the good man she always told me to pray for. Things were going well. I went back and forth to New York a few times and met his family. That was a turning point not only was I falling for X-Man, but his family too. There was closeness in his family that was missing in mine, and I thought it was wonderful. In X-Man family, there seemed to be nonjudgmental people and that was not the case in mine. They accepted me for my imperfect self.

Over time, my mother started to not like X-Man or me living with her. I was working and going to school, so there were times that X-Man was home more than I was. I noticed also him getting closer to another female student at school. Of course, X-Man told me that was just a girl at school helping him in math and reassured me that I had nothing to worry about. This was the first time that I questioned him and another female about their relationship. I had to ask her for myself, because what X-Man was telling me just didn't feel so honest.

One day she called our house phone and I picked up. When she asked for him and I said he wasn't there, she hung up, but I had to know. I called her back. I made sure to stay calm, but I asked her what was going on. I told her that if she thought he was just living here with me and my mother and nothing was going on, that she was sadly mistaken. She started crying, and that sealed it for me. I knew he was talking to her behind my back. I told her that I was sorry that she was upset, and that if she wanted him, she could have him.

After we hung up, I wondered if I should stay with him or let him go. Friends told me he was up to no good, but I chose to stay with him. Around this time, my mother told us both that we had to move out. I went to live with a female friend of mine, and so did he. Crazy as this sounds, but I believed him telling me it was just a roof over his head and that he still wanted to be with me. The fear of losing someone who was supposed to be in love with me just as much as I loved him kept me in the relationship. I figured if I kept loving him, it would work; he would love me completely back.

How many times do we think that if we just love someone hard enough, the other person will reciprocate? I definitely did. I always was taught to treat people how you want to be treated. Isn't it supposed to be like that too when you're in LOVE? It also is easy to give opinions to someone else in a situation but living in that situation you sometimes do the opposite of the advice you would give someone else.

It was tough finding time to see each other. We lived in two different places, went to school and worked, and he didn't have a car; not the easiest way to conduct a relationship. X-Man and I finally came across a one-bedroom apartment that we could move into and be together. I thought that would solve all my issues. I continued to tell myself, "If you just treat him like you want to be treated, it will work." I was still working one and even two jobs at one point while going to community college. X-Man was still in school as well and was working as a counselor at a local community center for kids.

In 2004 I remember going to the mall because I just wasn't feeling like myself, and for a woman, shopping can cure it temporarily. I noticed my normal size wasn't fitting and that made me wonder if there was a possibility that I could be pregnant. On the way home,

I stopped at a drug store. Sure enough, the test came back positive and I cried like a baby. So many thoughts went through my mind.

#1 I'm not married yet.

#2 What is going to be his reaction?

#3 Am I really ready? I have to be now.

#4 Will this make us closer?

#5 He is good with all the kids he works with?

#6 Was this really what I wanted in the situation I was in?

I always wanted to be a mom and always told myself no matter what if I ended up pregnant for my actions, then I would take care of my responsibility.

I told X-Man when he came home that day and he tried to talk to me about having an abortion and how we were only in our relationship for about two years. This was one decision I was strong in and told him that he did not have to stay with me just because I was pregnant. During this time, he was also offered a chance to play basketball and receive his education through another college. I told X-Man to go take that opportunity to further his education, and that the baby and I would visit him. He turned it down for whatever reason.

As many times as I heard that we were not ready to have a baby, I knew I had to take care of this responsibility. I chose life and to have my first-born son. As the pregnancy went on, I tried to get X-Man to commit completely. I was so happy about becoming a mom. Looking back, there is a joy you get knowing that that this life that will love you forever because you are that child's parent. I thought this would make X-Man and I grow closer as well. He worked with kids of various ages every day, so I figured he was going to be a good dad. He stuck around, and our first son was born.

Before he was born, we moved into a two-bedroom apartment and the feeling of being a family began to sink in. Given the fact that X-Man didn't really want this life (at least not yet), I suppose I shouldn't have been surprised when he got physical with me for the first time. It was less than a year after the baby was born, and we argued. I was cleaning out my closet of all the clothes that I could no longer fit. I can't exactly remember what it was we disagreed about, but at one point, he grabbed my arms and shook me back and forth. When I told him to leave, he responded with 'I didn't put my hands on you, I just shook you a little.' I told him that is one thing I am truly against and will not accept. He apologized, and I accepted. The physical abuse got tucked away, and out came the emotional abuse.

Emotional Abuse is defined as "any act including confinement, isolation, verbal assault, humiliation, intimidation, infantilization, or any other treatment which may diminish the sense of identity, dignity, and self-worth. Emotional abuse is known to leave more scars on a person than physical abuse. I am a witness—it HURTS.

As life continued and a baby being born in 2005, shouldn't we be thinking about really committing to each other? As a new mother I was putting a lot of attention into our new baby. This was new for the both of us and I guess the little attention X-Man was getting was not enough. His reaction was to entertain other women (he always told me they were just friends, but I never met them) and deflect from that by criticizing everything I did or tried to do (why don't you help clean up this or cook that?).

On X-Man's birthday, I decided to make his favorite chocolate cake. This was my first-time baking. I even called his mother to make sure I was doing it correctly. Well, it didn't come out the best; let's just say the icing was the only thing holding it together. After a few days went by and the cake barely was eaten, X-Man decided to just throw the cake in the trash. He said it was because it wasn't going to get eaten anyway, but the truth was, he wanted to use that badly made cake to hurt me. After getting so much criticism from making that cake and other meals, I began to not like cooking at all. I can honestly say that I probably began to lose myself after being put down about things, and because of that, the baby got even more of my attention. I just figured if I just continue to try to make this work and showed him that I knew how to make someone happy, it would get better.

I didn't want to lose myself completely though. Even with a baby, I still graduated from community college. I finished my Associates degree with an A.S. in Office Administration and wanted to do more. X-Man and I talked about what each of us could do to better ourselves and our family. I told X-Man I wanted to take online courses and get my bachelor's degree, and that he should complete his Associate's or find something he loved and make a career of it. It sounded good when we talked about it, but when we had to put it into practice, something went wrong.

I was a mother, working full time, student and a partner in a relationship. Something was bound to get less attention, and it turned out to be the relationship.

I thought we had this understanding. He knew I was doing this for our family, and that it would take me putting in time to do it. There were plenty of nights when I spent all night studying or writing a paper instead of giving X-Man that attention. Instead of telling me how he felt, I guess X-Man chose to look for the attention he was craving in other places. I found text messages in his phone, and when I asked about them, I got that "Oh that is just a friend" line. I tucked that away as not being serious and kept telling myself that the hard work I was putting in for us would eventually pay off. It took longer than I would have liked, but I did receive my B.S. in Business Administration in May 2011 and got promoted to the finance department at my job. My drive for learning and wanting to better my education is the one thing that I did not lose.

Unfortunately, I lost important things in other areas of myself. Things like my self-worth and self-control were slowly being taken away and I was not even aware. I just remember thinking that if I showed X-Man how much I cared about our future, then there would possibly be marriage. I brought it up, and some would say I gave him an ultimatum (I didn't see it that way). I brought it up to him because I wanted him to fully commit to JUST ME. I explained to him that I didn't understand why it was so hard for him to take that step since we already lived together, had a baby together and paying bills together. My view of marriage was two people truly committing to each other and compromising when they are faced with challenges. I saw us as doing that already, and I wanted the full commitment of marriage.

X-Man finally agreed with me and the proposal happened at Yankee stadium in front of a couple of hundred people, something I didn't expect from him. I thought this was the start of something great. He proposed in 2007, and the wedding was planned for August 2009. It didn't happen because I caught him again texting and calling another woman – cheating. I gave him the silent treatment for a day or two while I thought through what I wanted. It wasn't that tough to figure out in my mind. I wanted my family to work. I wanted to finish the wedding planning that I was doing and enjoying, and I wanted to marry the father of my child. I tried the stay calm approach and asked him a simple question: do you want your family or not? Again, he chose his family. He chose us, and I believed him.

June 5, 2010 was a happy day in my life. All the hard work and planning had paid off. We had fun – one big party – but to me, it was more than that. I was happy because I had all the things that I dreamed of since I was a little girl. I was a mom. I had a promising job that I was employed at for six years, and now I was a wife. We had promised each other that we wouldn't change. We would treat each other the same. We either shouldn't have made that promise, or we should have set some boundaries and restrictions to go with it.

I never thought I would be with someone controlling and not know it. I made compromises and gave up some things that made me happy so that I could be a better girlfriend and then wife. I figured giving up my happiness to make someone else happy was right. Boy, I was wrong! I missed things like playing a sport, being active or exercising, girl time with friends without him getting upset and keeping God actively first in our lives and household. I yearned for those things and did not get them.

There were other things X-Man didn't give me either. Our relationship was missing something. I wanted that spouse who knew how to build me up when I was feeling down, and the more I noticed that I didn't have that spouse in X-Man, the more I began to lose myself. I thought hard about this, but I don't recall X-Man every saying "I'm proud of you for achieving your bachelor's degree while working a full-time job." If he said it, I didn't feel it was heartwarming and genuine because I wouldn't have forgotten that feeling. I craved it way too much to forget if I'd ever gotten that from him.

X-Man must have felt he was missing something from me as well – why else would he have looked for it elsewhere the way he did? Looking back, it was clear that he took his frustration out on me in criticizing me constantly. This wasn't clean to his liking or that wasn't clean at all. My cooking wasn't any good, I heard that enough times until I let him cook all the time and then he complained that I never cooked. I heard that kind of stuff so much I thought it was the norm. I wanted my marriage to work so badly I sold myself short. Looking back discussing what is needed with your partner is so important. Be aware of your love languages to share with your partner and be ready to receive their love languages.

Being married had me thinking about having a second baby. I enjoyed the feeling of having a helpless baby around, depending on Mommy for everything, and I craved it again. I thought that having a new baby in the house would make us happy again. X-Man and I talked about having another baby, and there were times when I wasn't sure if I would be the best mother to two children. I hoped I wouldn't show one child favoritism over the other.

I also had to deal with health issues while trying to get pregnant. I have Basedow's disease (also known as Grave's disease), which is an immune system disorder that affects the thyroid gland and must be treated with medication or removed. It was causing me to have rapid heartbeats, hand tremors, trouble sleeping and nervous excitability very frequently. I described it as feeling like I was going through menopause in my twenties. Once I got my thyroid under control, I had to take medicine to even get pregnant. It took a while, but baby #2 was born in February of 2012 and things did begin to change.

X-Man handled it badly. All the attention he got was more focused on doing baby things or on our older son. He acted jealous of the time I spent on the children, and he focused his bad attitude on me. X-Man fell back into old habits- since he felt like he wasn't getting enough attention at home, he looked for it elsewhere. This is when I started to realize that he was emotionally abusive. There were plenty of times when he talked about how any woman would love to have him and would appreciate all the things he did. Those famous words pushed my self-esteem lower and lower, but I was the only one adjusting and trying to make things better.

I worked full time and came home to two kids just like him, but X-Man still thought we should be having the same amount of sex we did before we were parents. I tried talking to him about it. I explained that I was tired after working and then coming home to the boys, and that X-Man staying up till 1-2 a.m. was just not doable for me anymore. I asked him to come to bed earlier and then go back to his video games after if he wanted to stay up so late. I tried telling him that intimacy and foreplay begins during the day with a phone call while at work, a sexy text message, or anything that said he was thinking of me all day long and not just at night. He heard me but didn't listen.

How can you be married and still lonely? How can you be in the same house with another adult and feel invisible? It sounds impossible, and I didn't believe it until I lived it. By year three of our marriage, there were plenty of nights I cried myself to sleep praying to **God that this can't be it, this can't be love**. For the first time in my life I was surrounded by other human beings but felt at times I was invisible to the only other adult in the house. X-Man kept up his routine of complaints – not enough sex, complaints about my cooking and cleaning, not enough affection, not understanding why I wanted to start exercising on the regular. It felt to me like X-Man did things just for us to fight so he could have excuses to stay out of the house or find someone new to call or text.

I started to think I needed a therapist because of this. *Depression is real* and can take a person days, weeks or sometimes months to get out of. I sought out a therapist because the feeling of loneliness had found its way into my spirit; the put downs began to sink into my mind and I started to believe all those things he told me. I finally got to where I wanted to make myself better as a way to make my marriage better. Instead of not exercising because of him, I started going to the gym both to lose my baby weight and to exercise my spirit as well. Working out made me feel better, and therapy helped me even more along those lines. I also decided to grow further in my religion. To read the bible more, to worship more and to speak to a pastor about the decisions I was making and path that I was on.

X-Man embarrassed me one particular day; I never felt so low. It was a normal day at work for me, and it was raining on and off that day. X-Man knew it was my payday and we had made a prior agreement about him paying a ticket for me and I would give it back. I didn't think anything of it – we were married. I thought that he knew if I had extra money, then he had extra money. But that only went one way.

He pestered me with phone calls all day about him wanting the money for the ticket. I was appalled because priorities of our bills coming first did not seem to matter. I did have cash on me this particular morning and I let him know that. He kept telling me he wanted it all. He arrived at my job just as I was leaving for lunch break with my co-worker to go to the gym. X-Man had such an evil look on his face that I don't remember seeing before (at least not aimed at me). He only cracked the window enough for me to put the money through. He asked me if that was all of it and when I responded no, he threw it back at me in the rain. I couldn't believe what I had just witnessed. It felt like he had just spit on me and told me I'm not good enough. I held in the tears and went to the gym with my co-worker after he pulled off.

I wasn't at the gym five minutes before he started calling and texting me about how he ran out of gas. I ignored them. My first thought was well you shouldn't have been mean and ignorant and NOT take cash if you didn't have gas. I also thought to myself "Thank you God for that karma." My gut told me he was up to something else and that things were going to get worse. I then received threatening messages about how he was going to come to my job and make a scene if I did not give him the complete amount of money that he was looking for. This really hurt me and put me in a place where I honestly didn't know what to do. I was with my employer for almost 10 years by this time and was the financial head of our household. I didn't want my job in jeopardy because of my deranged husband. I was forced into a situation of giving him what he wanted—or he was going to jeopardize something I had worked so hard for.

I gave in, as so many victims to abuse do. We give in to giving an abuser what they want thinking it will make the situation better for us, but we still end up getting hurt in the end.

I left the cash I tried giving him before and my debit card for the rest in my car so he could finally get what he wanted. When he returned my debit card, he then told me that I was going to have to figure how to get our oldest son off the bus today because he would not be available to do it. That really pissed me off. What was he up to and where was he going now that he had cash in his hand? I remember going into mom mode calling the school and a friend to see if Baby#1 could come to her house after school and I would get him from there. I remember X-Man's mother calling after I had picked up the kids and I was at the gas station and I couldn't even speak to her because I was crying hysterically, telling her he was just so mean.

Well, the nastiness was not over. I walked into our home started dinner while the kids occupied themselves with cartoons and homework. I decided to take my cardigan off and hang it in my closet upstairs to only notice that none of my other clothes were hanging in the closet. I checked the second closet and my clothes were not there either. I then realized that it was raining outside, and I hoped that all my clothes were not outside in the backyard. They weren't out there, which left one other place – the basement. This basement was not finished. It was just storage space with a washer and dryer. X- Man threw all my clothes all over the basement floor. I tried to call X-Man several times with no answer. I left messages asking how he could just up and leave his wife and children and not care at all. I tried to stay calm for the sake of my children, but after I put them to bed, I cried myself to sleep.

The next morning, I noticed an email from the bank regarding unusual activity at a hotel in New York. I'd called his parents when I noticed he was gone, and they had no idea he was in the same state with them. At this point I wanted X- Man to stay where he was. Enough was enough. X-Man returned home after speaking with his parents and said he needed some time away. At this point, I felt like I was living with a roommate instead of being in a marriage. I thought it was either going to get better or get worse, nothing in between.

A few days later, X-Man came home from work expecting sex. I was astonished; how could he expect anything the way our marriage was? After I asked him if he was serious, he looked me straight to my face and told me that the girl I found him talking to this time was the one he was leaving me for. A light bulb went off; I knew right then that this was no longer a marriage, if it ever was.

I finally got the courage to tell him to leave, that we needed to separate. He agreed but then by the end of the conversation, he changed his tune. He said nope, sorry, you're stuck with me until (younger son) turns sixteen. This seemed so odd, but I was so drained from the emotional rollercoaster that I just ended my night praying that same prayer I always said and going to sleep. "**God this can't be it, this can't be love**."

At this point something had to change, so I decided to start with myself. I figured I could change myself and the marriage would work or change myself and it would be better for me by myself. Either way, I needed things to be better. I looked for a therapist to help me work on my thoughts. I knew that at this time in my life, I was not emotionally or physically where I wanted to be as a woman. I felt a need to work from the inside out; my self-esteem had been dragged to probably its lowest point ever.

When I shared my thoughts with my therapist, it was amazing. I heard a total stranger tell me that how I was being treated was not normal, and it made me feel different; I felt better. I learned that I was trying so hard to force the love between me and X-Man that I forgot how to love myself first. My self-esteem, my sense of worth slowly returned.

As I began to feel better, I suggested to X-Man that he should either join me at therapy or see a separate therapist. At the end of the day, I knew he was the father of my children that I had feelings for, and that he deserved a chance to feel better too. I believe that everyone is capable of becoming a better version of themselves if they put effort into it. Unfortunately, he didn't believe in telling his personal business to someone who did not know us, and he refused both suggestions.

As I continued to feel better from the inside out, my relationship with my husband became worse. He moved from mind games to physical threats. X-Man tried to force me to give him oral sex.

Now I understand that in any marriage, there are times when one spouse wants to be more physical than the other, and when that happens, the spouse who isn't feeling it usually gives in. This was something completely different. We had just had an argument about him texting another woman and he wanted to get some. I said to X-Man "Are you SERIOUS?" I had to explain to him that intimacy doesn't work that way. He grabbed me by the shoulders, pulled me close to him and told me that I was his wife and therefore I was supposed to do whatever he asked. I noticed a look in his eyes that I'd never seen before, and it scared me. I said to myself "God, please protect me."

Because I did not give in to having oral sex, he chose to threaten me with a hanger. He raised it to my head and demanded I give him my wedding ring. He told me if I didn't give it to him, it was going to be a major problem. All I could think of were the two little boys sleeping in their rooms. If all X-Man wanted was a ring that was mine, a ring that was a materialistic item that symbolized commitment, oneness and love then, so be it. I let him have the ring.

This night was another eye opener for me. What was happening in my marriage? Of course, that was another night I cried myself to sleep praying to God that this can't be it, this can't be love. Here was another sign that maybe this was not my God given relationship. As usual, I wondered what to do next, and I did what I always did; pushed it aside. I figured I had to keep going for my kids' sake, so I tucked it away. I would get up in the morning, get dressed, go to work and smile, and hide the fact that my heart was breaking into a million pieces.

I am a thinker and a daydreamer, and in the back of my mind, I wondered what to do. I wondered if I should just keep my distance from X-Man and not do anything to trigger that anger that I previously had seen. I was in a relationship with someone and I felt lonelier than I had ever felt before. In all that, there was still a part of me that thought I could turn X-Man around and save my marriage. I did everything I could, but it only got worse.

I experienced my last physical altercation on a Friday morning. I was getting ready for work, and I thought he was too. However, I noticed that X-Man was packing enough clothes to go away for the weekend! We weren't doing so great at the time. I wouldn't have mind him going away, but I needed to know some things first.

I asked him where he was going and reminded him that we had bills to pay and responsibilities to the house. He told me to "shut up," and when I kept asking questions, it became "Shut the f%$! up!" I said one more thing and the next thing I knew, he grabbed me by the arm and tossed me across the bedroom. I tried to get up, and he pushed me back down! The third time I tried to get up, he pinned me down and yanked the ring off my finger (yes, the same ring he demanded before and then left for me to put back on).

I was so scared a punch was coming next, and that I'd end up knocked out or having to go to the hospital. I was screaming at the top of my lungs for him to get off me and get out, and all the while, our sons were in their bedrooms and my husband's nephew and his girlfriend were downstairs. It all happened at once- one of them knocked on the bedroom door and he yanked the ring off my finger and let me up at the same time. I ran to the bathroom crying and in disbelief that this had happened. I talked to my co-worker (who has become my best friend) and she told me to call the police. But all I could think about was the looks on my kids' faces when the police arrived to take their dad out of the house; I didn't call. I finally wiped my tears and left the bathroom, only to overhear X-Man talking to our oldest son, who was crying and so upset. His room was next to ours; he heard all the commotion and heard his mother screaming for his father to get off her.

I walked in to see tears on his face, and I tried to show him that Mommy was all right; I was only hurt on the inside. X-Man was telling our son stuff like this happened because Mommy did not love Daddy enough, Mommy did not listen, Mommy could have avoided this if she just stayed quiet when I asked her to and other lies and nonsense. I instantly had a flashback to my preteen years and how my stepfather treated my brother and me. When he was dating our mother, he was a different person. After they exchanged vows, he became mean, physically abusive and verbally cruel. He hit us, and also put us down with words. He told us all the time that we didn't do things right, which meant we didn't do them his way. Now here I was, twenty some years later, still feeling like that little girl. At that moment, all I could say to my son was "I am sorry you have witnessed all of this" and "X-Man this is not how you treat someone you love." I left the room thinking about the things that my son would have to listen to about his mom and realized that my children's lives just changed as well.

I still ended up going to work. Have you ever been numb to something that happens? That is how I got through that workday. I recall having a short moment in the bathroom but then I wiped the tears and went back to my desk as if I didn't experience something traumatic in my relationship. How did we get to this in our marriage? Or did I allow this to happen to myself? I was questioning myself as women always do, what did I do to deserve this? I did know that I did not want this to continue. I only could think about how I would like my children to grow up and become. I could not let this cycle continue.

Over the past years domestic violence has grown becoming an issue that is not just happening in our homes. Our society is now seeing it take place outside of individual homes and finally trying to speak out about it. The topic of domestic violence has always been something that women or men just did not speak about. Majority of the time society has been scared to discuss it. Well its time. Statistics say that around the world, one in every three women have been beaten, coerced into sex or otherwise abused in their lifetime. Sadly, the abuser is mostly a family member. Domestic Violence is the leading cause of injury to women - more than car accidents, mugging, and rapes combine. Women and men are abused daily and sometimes killed due to domestic violence. It is not always about a man abusing a woman, it could also be a family member being abused by another family member. The awareness needs to spread so the person being abused will not be afraid to tell someone. This is an act that has no preference. It can happen to anyone. You do not have to have a marital status to make a complaint. Let's hope that if there are signs of domestic violence before marriage that the person can ESCAPE it before getting married. If you're reading this and have been a victim of domestic violence or know someone who has please make sure you know that "This is NOT real LOVE." It's time to ESCAPE these fears of not speaking out and help others learn how to ESCAPE them as well.

You are not experiencing Love when you are being abused. How do I know what domestic abuse looks like? Because I believe that Love is patient, Love is kind, Love is disagreeing with someone's point without saying unkind words or being physical with them. Yes, words can be just as hurtful as or more hurtful than someone physically abusing you. This is known as mental and emotional abuse. Mental and emotional abuse for most couples is worse than physical abuse. When you first acknowledge that you are being mistreated/abused please take a moment and ask yourself "Is this REAL LOVE?" The answer should be NO. The majority of the time, an abuser will start with mental abuse; wants to know what you are doing every second of the day. It will seem like every second of the day if it is every hour. They will accuse you of being unfaithful all the time, get angry in a way that is frightening, humiliate you in front of others and make decisions for you that you can make for yourself. You will question your decision-making because your ideas are "not good enough" and are unrecognized. Your opinions don't matter. These are just a few signs of mental and emotional abuse. If you begin to recognize this abuse and disagree in any way, you may then experience the physical abuser. Items being thrown, a push, slap or punch, or being assaulted with a weapon are all signs that you have been physically abused by someone.

You see, the victim must understand that this abuse that they have experienced has probably made them loose the love they have for them self. I suggest first recognize that the love for yourself has been lost and that is needs to be reestablished. Sit and ponder in a peaceful place and think about the things you use to enjoy doing. What were those things that you liked to do because it made you feel good, strong, empowered and beautiful? The abuser has stepped in and has only made the way you think, feel and love about yourself nonexistent by putting you down with their words or even their hands. Find that SELF LOVE. Begin to change your thoughts about yourself. None of the put downs that you are experiencing are true nor are they normal for a healthy relationship. Dig deep and begin to plan your ESCAPE.

This *Power and Control Wheel* is a good example of things that happen in a coercive relationship.

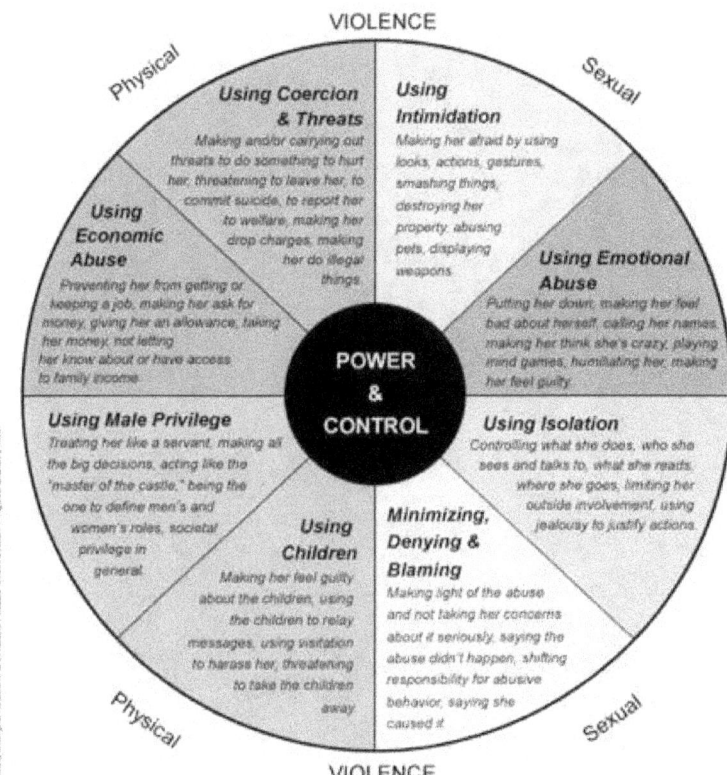

Evaluate your relationship and compare it with the *Power and Control Wheel*, and be conscious of what type of relationship you are in. Make the necessary changes or remove yourself completely.

EXIT PLAN

How do I get out of this abusive relationship? Why did I stay in this relationship?

The first reason why I stayed is because I did not like the idea of having my children grow up without a father in the home like I did. I had to compare my desire to keep my family together with their needs. I remember my brother and me wanting to run away from living with my stepfather and mother. We wanted to escape because no one understood how we were living under someone who was so unkind. I asked myself, "do I want my sons to feel the same way?" I didn't want them to think they should run away because Mommy and Daddy are always arguing with each other. As a child, my brother and I couldn't understand why our mom was getting verbally and emotionally abused by that man and letting him do the same to us. As a child in this situation I couldn't escape by myself my mother also had to want to escape as well.

Now I was an adult in the same shoes as my mother was, and I refused to wait until my children wanted to escape. I decided to do it for them. I wondered if I could make it financially alone. *Oh, wait, I was already handling the majority of the financial responsibilities anyway.*

The thought of being alone after 13 years with someone honestly was a little scary. How would it be not to have him there physically anymore? How would others see me? Would anyone else want me? Would they then wonder what happened? I didn't want to hear stuff like "You guys seem so happy." "You guys were a great couple." Trust me, everything that you see on the outside is not always what is happening behind closed doors. I thought about these things and then thought, *I must escape!!! Who am I? I have to ESCAPE and find out who I really am.*

I made my final decision because I did not want to stay and see if the physical abuse would get worse, or the emotional rollercoaster would continue. At first, I thought asking him to leave would be enough, but he only left for two- three days and came back. After a few times of this, I told him that wasn't enough and that I needed him completely away--as in no longer living in the house I found and mostly paid for. I needed for the first time in a long time to put my happiness and my expectations before others.

I ended up discussing this with my therapist and best friend and they both agreed that I should get a Protection From Abuse (PFA) order saying that he could not be around me or the house. I filed for a PFA mostly to get the space I needed. I did not keep him from seeing his sons, but I needed time to clear my head and figure out what was best for myself and my kids. With him no longer in the home, I was able to see that the expectations of our relationship on my part were not matching the reality. I realized that X-Man was truly unhappy over those last few years. Without him around arguing with me daily and criticizing everything I said and did; I was able to take a step back towards the old me. Of course, he tried to come back on many occasions, but I was very clear that if there was any chance of that happening, changes would have to be made. He asked me stuff like "How would you know if I'm not there for you to see?" I was not falling for it this time. I told him I would know because your actions would be different. He did not understand it but let me explain to you what I meant. His words when he spoke to me would not sound like words of anger. He would pick up the children and help me financially with them without me asking, and just overall do and speak with generosity. He didn't show any of those signs while he was out of the home, so why should I expect to see change if I let him return?

X-Man even had the nerve to tell me "If you don't know me by now then you just don't know me. I don't need to change."

I decided I was not taking the chance on letting him come back. I wanted BETTER, I deserved BETTER. I hated to be one of those statistics (an African American family that broke up due to divorce), but a girl deserves to be happy. We all deserve to be happy and that means to find TRUE LOVE.

Don't be afraid to ESCAPE from something that isn't REAL and be alone.

An exit plan is usually not going to happen overnight—it's a process. Victims who are financially abused cannot just walk away because the finances of the family are run by the other party. It can take months sometimes for this person to finally escape. My advice to you is to confide in someone that you truly trust. If they can help you escape financially, then take it. Don't be filled with so much pride that you are willing to put your life and sanity on the line. If that person is not able to help you financially, then every chance you get, please put some money away that your abuser is not able to find. The sooner you can escape, the better.

AFTERMATH

I am divorced and standing in my singleness. I am the happiest I have ever been. I wake up happy to be alive, thrilled about living and being a service to others. I love to show kindness to people that I don't even know.

While going through this process, I realized I had to get real with myself. I had to look in the mirror and get honest. I asked myself "When did you fall in love with yourself?" You see, for the first time I could stare myself in the mirror and not look past the person that was looking at me but look her directly in her eyes. I realized that I didn't start to fall in love with her until I was in my 33rd year of living. I was so busy trying to please and do for others that I didn't take a moment to really look me in the face and lock eyes. Now I am completely in love with me, and I know that I will not make the same mistakes I made in the past. *The one who gets wisdom loves life; the one who cherishes understanding will soon prosper*. Proverbs 19:8 NIV.

During my first year of freedom, I fell deeper in love with me. I found the things that made me happy and looked back over previous years to see that God had a plan for me all along. Example: we had to unexpectedly move out of our prior home due to mold. My children have asthma—I was not having that. I found us a new home directly around the corner from where we were already living. When I walked in to view it, something came over me and made it just feel like it was home. At the current time X-Man was working 2nd shift and I was working day shift. I scheduled the lease signing for the afternoon, on my lunch break and before he had to go to work. The morning of, I received a text message from him asking for the address. I sent it back. Something in my gut, that sixth sense, my intuition, told me that something was off.

My lunch break came, I got there early, and my husband was nowhere to be found. I sat in my car on the phone with my best friend crying he wouldn't answer texts or calls. I told her this and wondered out loud what kind of man would leave his wife alone to sign a lease for their family. I knew I couldn't pass up this opportunity on this place; it felt like home when I walked in. In that moment, I felt the Holy Spirit tell me that it is okay I am with you. It was time for me to go into the building, so I wiped my tears, picked my head up and told my best friend thank you for being on the phone with me. As we hung up, I told God thank You for being with me and whatever is in Your plan is

what will happen. *For I know the plans I have for you,"
declares the Lord, "plans to prosper you and not to harm
you, plans to give you hope and a future.* - Jeremiah
29:11 NIV

I did not know if they would approve me for the home on my one income. I made enough alone, but I had originally put both incomes on the application. I walked in sat down and got everything I wanted! The gentleman approved me to sign on just my income, agreed to put in a washer and dryer for no extra cost and allowed me to sign the lease only in my name. The *Holy Spirit* told me not only to do that, but to only list myself and my children as inhabitants. I didn't know what would happen in the next few months, but God did. Four months later, the physical abuse came with the altercation in the bedroom, and I had enough. I decided I did not want this to get worse for me or my children and I wanted to live. Putting him out was so much easier since his name was never on the lease!

Even though it has been rough financially, I am getting me back; nothing else matters. I have become stronger than I have ever been, relying on my faith and the promise that God gives each one of us. It was also rough emotionally. Let me tell you, in the first year of being divorced, emotions were all over the place at times. Loneliness kicked in and I was sad seemingly out of nowhere. I was crying about being single, the struggle of being a single mom, if I would ever heal enough that someone else would want me. Then I thought about what it would be like if I would have stayed. I would still have ALL these same emotions plus him putting his hands on me. I thought about that old saying, "You can do bad all by yourself." I found out that if I worked on loving me more and more, those emotions faded away. My happiness and my children's happiness are what matters to me the most. Being free is the most rewarding feeling that I have experienced from escaping. I feel as though I shine brighter than I have ever before. *Be strong and courageous. Do not be afraid or terrified because of them, for the Lord your God goes with you; he will never leave you nor forsake you.* - Deuteronomy 31:6 NIV

I saw the changes in my children too. I watched their behavior before and after being separated. When there is abuse, children are often afraid to ask questions because they think they did something wrong and fear getting yelled at or hit for asking anything. This has actually brought my children and I closer we tend to talk more. I remind them that I can show them how to love. Love with their actions not just words. I will show them that hardwork and determination of your dreams will not be an easy task but it is doable and can happen. I will be an example that faith and love in God will make all things possible.

FAITH & SPIRITUALITY

You are probably wondering why this chapter is in this book. It has everything to do with how I escaped. If I did not have faith that God could help me get out of my situation, I would be still in it. Faith is having complete trust and confidence in something you cannot see. My situation was nothing like I imagined or wanted it to be. When you're in your lowest point of your life, it is hard to speak to another imperfect human being. Having faith in someone greater than me who is perfect, who cannot and will not steer me in the wrong direction saved me. Having faith that my situation would change for the better and that I would change too felt a lot better than staying in it.

I grew up Methodist with a family that went to church every Sunday, and as a child, you did too. I strayed away as a teenager, but always believed in God and that He is greater than me and I am His child. After my first child and shortly after losing my father, I decided to go back to my home church where I grew up. It was a small United Methodist church in the neighborhood where I had spent my teenage years. That Sunday it was just my son and me, and I can remember it like yesterday. As I sat in church and saw my grandfather singing in the choir, I began to feel that sense of the *Holy Spirit* that was missing. I cried at the altar as I rededicated my life to Christ. I cried knowing that not having an intentional relationship with God was what I was missing. I decided at that moment to no longer run away from the relationship with my heavenly Father. I needed to build myself up with God, run back to Him. It's always a learning process. No one is perfect. To this very moment I ask God to help me through life daily. I know that I made a promise to God that I want to keep. I promised I would try to be more like Him every day and to introduce my children to the One who will always be there.

I came across a church in the city I live in and as soon as I walked in with my first-born son, I felt welcome. You're probably wondering where he is at this particular time and if we were still together. Yes, we were together and later married, but not in this particular church. X-Man did not like to attend church as much as I did. He would be considered a holiday church member. The closer and closer I got in my relationship with God, the more distant X-Man became. I then began to realize that God had a plan the entire time. He wrote this story. He knew that I picked X-Man to be my husband; He did not bring him to me.

When things between myself and X-Man went downhill and we separated, I spoke to the pastor of the church and made him aware of my situation. I wanted to speak to him because I made vows to God and my husband till death do us part. I also began to get monthly counseling from a minister. I wanted to know that, in my choosing to stay or no longer stay in my marriage, that I did everything I could to make it work. It crossed my mind plenty of times that I joined this church as a married woman. My children were baptized together while we were married, and now, I'm a divorced single mother of two boys. What would people say? Would they wonder what my story was?

This thought crossed my mind, but I needed to get spiritually fed on a weekly basis. Everyone has their reasons for attending church. Some like to do it and others don't because they may feel the church just collects money. I personally attend my church because the pastor is a great teacher. I have great support in other women and men who encourage and lift me up. I have a handful of church family members who I have asked to adopt me and my sons into their families like we have adopted them into ours. Coming out of an abusive situation, you always need others who support you and see something in you that you may not see in yourself at times. God knew that I would go through the emotional and then physical abuse before finally saying, "No more!" God knew what was going to push me closer to Him. I know that Mark 11:24 NIV says, *"Therefore I tell you, whatever you ask for in prayer, believe that you have received it, and it will be yours."* My prayer to God that the situation that I was in couldn't be love was accurate, and I know that I was taken out of it to find love. Not love in a human being but to completely love God and myself.

I mentioned that I was raised in a United Methodist church, and I am still in the Methodist religion. I attend an AME (African Methodist Episcopal) church now, and I live my Christianity through Methodist practices and beliefs. On the first Sunday of each month we have Holy Communion; we recite the apostle creed and the AME motto: "God our Father, Christ our Redeemer, the Holy Spirit our Comforter, Humankind our Family." Every day I ask to be more like Jesus and practice the fruit of the spirit.

But the fruit of the Spirit is love, joy, peace, forbearance, kindness, goodness, faithfulness, gentleness and self-control. Against such things there is no law. - Galatians 5:22-23

Spirituality is not the same as religion. A person can refer to him or herself as a spiritual person but not hold the loving presence of God in them. There are groups that call themselves spiritual groups, but who practice unkindness to others that are different than themselves. Spirituality to me means believing in something greater than yourself and accepting that you are on this Earth for a reason. Trust your intuition to lead you to your purpose, and accept it and act on it, and in the end, it will be worth every minute to hear our Creator say, "Well done."

There are some things I would like to encourage you with that I have encouraged myself with to live a healthy spiritual life:

- *Accept what has happened to you in the past and know there are better things ahead when you move forward.* ***Let it GO.***

- ***Self-acceptance.*** Accept your flaws. Work on them but remember no one is perfect.

- ***Forgive.*** You will be at peace when you forgive yourself and others.

- ***Be Positive.*** Speaking positively to yourself to yourself and others is so important. You can learn something good out of every situation if you focus on the positive aspect.

- ***Encourage others.*** Lift them up, but do not wish to be in their shoes. Your story is a wonderful story and will help someone else. Don't be ashamed of what you have been through.

- ***Surround yourself with like-minded people.*** Keep people around you who want to grow and who have accepted their flaws; they are working on them and have goals for themselves and others. Who you surround yourself with sometimes determines who you will become. When you surround yourself with others that are always complaining, arguing with others and not trying to become better, there is a good chance you will start to do the same.

After getting out of my marriage, there were still times of weeping to God. This weeping was not the same weeping that I was doing in my marriage. It was more like "I am sorry, Lord. Now look what I have gotten myself into. I am a single mom with two children. I accept this journey that I have and want to fulfill my purpose that You have put before me, but what is it and how do I do it? "

One night I was sleeping well. Nothing had been weighing on my mind prior to sleeping this night, but I was awakened anyhow. I've learned that if you wake up in between the hours of three and four a.m., it is known as the Trinity hours; during that time, be sure to listen to the Holy Spirit. This night I woke up during the Trinity hours, and as soon as I was awakened, I said "Yes, Lord."

I didn't think I had anything on my mind worrying me, but then questions crossed my mind. Did I make the right choice in getting divorced? Am I making the right decisions right now? I felt like a little child being awakened for something bad. Then, as if the Holy Spirit was sitting in the room with me on my bed, He said "Did I ever steer you wrong?" As that "No" came out, I knew that maybe He appeared to tell me that He has me and that He is keeping me from any harm or any more setbacks. That tells me everything that I am feeling and doing will work out and work for my good.

THE NOW

As much as I want to tell you that I have met my Prince Charming, my Boaz, my King; I cannot tell you that. I can tell you that I found love for MYSELF. I love ME more than I ever have. I smile because I am not the same person that I used to be. I am learning and accepting myself for who I am. That way I will be ready to share myself with that special person when he comes along. I also feel that I will know now exactly what I want from a life partner.

I am a single mother of two boys that I love and take care of every day. There is a quote: "Men are what their mothers make them." I believe this quote is accurate. And vice versa for daddies and their daughters. I know that I cannot raise my sons to be men, but I can raise them and share with them how a woman wants to be treated and loved. Raising children with a spouse is not easy so raising my sons without one has me at times on my knees praying and crying to do the best job I can. I want them to see that faith in God will get you through the good and bad times. *Now faith is confidence in what we hope for and assurance about what we do not see.* Hebrews 11:1NIV.

Having a good support system is imperative. Sometimes this may not just mean family. For me it has been friends and my church family. I want to leave a legacy of what it is to love others as yourself, to be kind always, to take responsibility for your actions and be humble with the gifts God has given you to share with the world.

I want to be an example to the next teenager in a relationship or the next battered wife to let her know that she doesn't have to stay. I am doing things I would never have thought I would be doing and completely loving myself from the top of my head to the bottom of my feet first. I am an advocate for the Delaware Coalition Against Domestic Violence; I am an active member for my task force, which is under the coalition. I speak and interact with women who are in or are trying to get out of abusive relationships. I want to remind them they are good enough and that they can escape and be free. I have learned things that have helped me heal, and I want to share with others.

I use my work experience to help, as well. Having worked in the field of finance for a few years now helps me help abuse victims in a special way. I go to non-profit organizations specifically for women in domestic abuse to speak encouraging words to them about financial management. I want to encourage them and show them I made it and they can too. I have gotten certified in a life coaching/soul speaking course to guide others to find themselves and to pursue their purpose in life. My love of exercise and living healthy has not only turned into something that I do for myself for most of the week, but it has led me to become a fitness trainer. I want to go further and receive my Master of Science in Human Nutrition. When you're healthy in your mind, body and soul, nobody can take your power away easily from you.

I encourage you to have faith and remove yourself from any abusive relationship, whether it is with your spouse, boyfriend, girlfriend, family member, or a friend. Don't let someone else control you. I may not be exactly where I want to be at this present time, but I can certainly tell you that things are moving in the right direction. I recommend any woman or man who has been in an abusive relationship to seek ultimate love from a higher power. I know there is more than one religious belief in our society, but true love is accepted everywhere. It will only get better for you. Always remind yourself that you don't have to stay in any negative situation or hold on to any negative thoughts. Keep your mind full of positivity and your life will reflect that. Read a positive affirmation daily to remind yourself, "I am enough!" I have added a few of my favorite affirmations in hopes that one of them may become your favorite.

God Bless

QUOTES -- DAILY AFFIRMATIONS

I AM ENOUGH.

YOU ARE STONGER THAN YOU THINK. Be GREAT today. It's a new day.

SMILE it is contagious.

When I accept myself, I am freed from the burden of needing you to accept me. - Dr. Steve Maraboli

HEALTHY SELF HEAL THY SELF

"Difficult roads often lead to beautiful destinations." – Zig Ziglar

ATTRACT WHAT YOU WANT BY BEING WHAT YOU WANT.

LET IT GO.

Your PEACE is more important than driving yourself crazy trying to understand why something happened the way it did.

NOW that I am FREE, I can become who God has created me to be.

GOD PUT ME HERE.

BE CONFIDENT, BE HUMBLE. IT WAS ALL NECESSARY.

I CAN DO ANYTHING!

I Can Do ALL things through Christ who strengthens me. - Philippians 4:13 NIV

THANK YOU

Thank you to X-Man for this lesson learned. It has helped me to transform into the Woman God intended me to be. This story was not what I expected, but so necessary.

Thank you to my children for giving me a reason to look at something greater than just my life but to also look at their lives and know that I wanted more for them. The cycle will be broken.

There are a lot of names and I don't want to forget anyone so to each person that has held my hand, wiped tears, encouraged me to keep going, to be the leader I am supposed to be, I truly appreciate you and thank you from the bottom of my heart.

Do Nothing out of selfish ambition or vain conceit. Rather, in humility value others above yourselves, not looking to your own interest of the other. - Philippians 2:3-4 NIV

With Love,

Doritha N. Skinner

www.ingramcontent.com/pod-product-compliance
Lightning Source LLC
Chambersburg PA
CBHW051411290426
44108CB00015B/2248